This book belongs to:

....

Notes for Parents

- Encourage your child to find the picture stickers and answer the questions in the book.

- Use the gold star stickers to praise their successes, and to encourage their healthy habits.

- Fill in the 'I will' tasks on the wipe-clean reward chart, and the star targets and rewards. Your child will enjoy joining in with this too, particularly in choosing the rewards. They will love the sense of responsibility, and the excitement of working towards the treats they've chosen.

- Rewards need not be big, but they should be meaningful to your child: an extra bedtime story, baking a cake, going to the swimming pool or the park, having a friend to play, a pocket money treat – something that they enjoy, and that you feel is appropriate to what they have achieved.

- Always keep a positive attitude and remember to focus on their achievements. Never take away stickers or deny a reward that has been agreed and earned.

- Your child will soon appreciate that being healthy can be fun, and these positive early habits will help to encourage good health and fitness throughout their lives.

ISBN 978-1-84135-972-4

Copyright © Award Publications Limited

This edition first published 2012

Published by Award Publications Limited,
The Old Riding School, The Welbeck Estate,
Worksop, Nottinghamshire, S80 3LR

Printed in Malaysia

The Children's Book of HEALTHY HABITS

Sophie Giles

Illustrated by Kate Davies

AWARD PUBLICATIONS LIMITED

Everyone in the classroom has a cold. Colds are caused by germs, which spread easily if you don't cover your mouth and nose with a tissue when you cough or sneeze.

What gives you a cold?

Josh and Emily have colds. All the children make sure to use a tissue if they cough or sneeze, and to wash their hands often to stop germs spreading.

I use a tissue

How do you help to stop germs from spreading?

Kate doesn't always brush her teeth, and now they are starting to decay. Teeth need to be cleaned well every morning and night, or plaque can make them rot and give you smelly breath!

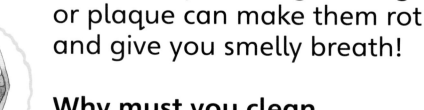

Why must you clean your teeth?

Now Kate brushes her teeth every day.
Her dentist says Kate won't need any
fillings this time because her teeth
are all nice and clean.

How do you clean
your teeth?

I clean
my teeth
well

Sam hates getting washed and never wants to have a shower or a bath. Nobody plays with him at school because of his bad odour.

Why does nobody want to play with Sam?

Sam's dad has bought him a fun towel and his own special soap. Bathtime is fun now and Sam never skips it. He has lots of friends to play with at school, too.

What is your favourite thing about bathtime?

I like bathtime

Jacob normally plays games on his computer and isn't used to running about outside. He is completely out of breath and he can't keep up with his teammates.

Why is Jacob out of breath?

Jacob goes for bike rides with his mum and dad instead of playing on his computer. Now that he is fitter, Jacob finds it easy to keep up on the football field.

How much exercise do you do?

I do plenty of exercise

Polly doesn't want to go in the bathroom yet because Matthew forgot to flush the toilet! He feels embarrassed and sneaks downstairs.

Why does Matthew feel embarrassed?

Now Matthew is more considerate of other people using the bathroom after him and always makes sure to flush the toilet once he has finished.

What should you do after flushing the toilet?

I wash my hands

Meena likes to have sleepover parties with her friends, but they don't like to stay at her house because her room is so messy and untidy.

Why do Meena's friends not like to sleep over?

Now that Meena keeps her room clean and tidy, her friends are always eager to come over to stay.

Do you keep your room neat and tidy?

Ethan loves fizzy drinks, but now he has toothache and headaches. The dentist says the sugar in the drinks is rotting his teeth and causing his headaches.

What is rotting Ethan's teeth?

Ethan has swapped his sugary drinks for water. His toothache and headaches have stopped and even his skin looks better!

I drink plenty of water

How much water do you drink each day?

Noah and Omar often stay up late watching television in their room. At school the next day they are tired and often get into trouble.

Why are the boys tired at school?

Mum has put the television downstairs and now the boys read books and comics at bedtime. After a good night's sleep they are happy and bright at school.

I get lots of sleep

How many hours do you sleep each night?

Suki's family eats a lot of fast food and ready-made meals. These meals are unhealthy and can contain a lot of salt and fats that are not good for you if you eat them often.

What meals are unhealthy?

Cooking meals using fresh ingredients can be lots of fun and is healthy for you, too. Fresh food is packed with the vitamins and goodness your body needs.

What healthy foods do you eat?

I eat healthy foods

Chloe is often tired in the afternoon because the energy from the sugary sweets and biscuits in her lunch is used up more quickly than energy from healthier foods.

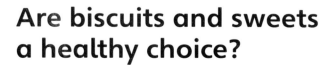

Are biscuits and sweets a healthy choice?

Chloe's class learns that our bodies need five portions of fruit and vegetables every day to help us stay healthy.
Chloe loves the carrots and fruit she now has in her lunchbox.

I eat my 5-a-day

Do you eat your 5-a-day?

Mum and Dad are trying to talk to Grandad, but it is too noisy! Mum has to shout because Tom's stereo is so loud and the twins are chasing through the house, disturbing everyone.

Why is Mum annoyed?

The children now understand that they must be considerate and think about the needs of others. Everyone is happier and there are fewer arguments.

Are you considerate towards others?

I think about the needs of others

Nihal is missing playing with his friends. He often forgets to wash his hands after going to the toilet. He bites his nails and the germs from his dirty hands have made him feel ill.

What has made Nihal ill?

Nihal has been out playing with his friends. He has stopped biting his nails and always washes his hands after using the toilet and before eating.

How do you wash your hands?

I use soap

Your **fitness** is a measure of how healthy you are, and depends on how much exercise you do. Exercise strengthens your heart, lungs and muscles. The more you do, the fitter you become.

Germs are tiny living cells that make you ill. Sometimes we call them 'bugs'. Germs give us upset tummies and colds.

When teeth **decay** it means they are rotting and dying away. A decaying tooth will have to be pulled out or filled by the dentist.

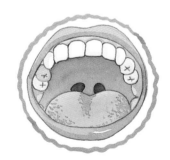

An **odour** is a smell. Usually the word odour is used to describe a bad smell. We can help to prevent body odour by washing every day.

Vitamins are the goodness in food. There are lots of different types, each helping your body in different ways. Vitamin C helps you to heal. Vitamin A helps you to see better at night.

To be **healthy** means you are not ill and that your body and mind are working properly. Being healthy makes you happy.

Being **considerate** means thinking how your actions will affect other people. Being inconsiderate can make others unhappy.

Habits are things that you do often, sometimes without even thinking. It is good to have healthy habits, such as washing your hands.

Quiz Time

You should wash your hands...
A. After going to the toilet
B. After having a bath
C. Before making a mud pie

Germs can make you feel...
A. Ticklish
B. Unwell
C. Hungry

Which is the odd one out?
A. Grilled chicken and rice
B. Baked potato and salad
C. Cheeseburger and chips

Vitamins are found naturally in...
A. The newspaper
B. The sock drawer
C. Fresh food

What would make you fitter?
A. Watching TV with friends
B. Playing chase with friends
C. Playing computer games

Sleep helps you to...
A. Refresh your body and mind
B. Learn to fly
C. Tidy your room

See if you can find the ten words hidden in the grid.

BATH   **GERM**
FAMILY   **HEALTHY**
HAPPY   **EXERCISE**
WASHING   **HABIT**
CLEAN   **TEETH**

Did you find them all?

Y	S	H	Y	B	Y	D	R	D	F
R	H	N	T	L	H	A	B	I	T
H	S	T	I	A	T	O	C	H	U
Z	A	M	L	E	B	E	L	G	A
A	A	P	E	A	Q	M	E	N	I
F	O	T	P	V	E	O	A	I	I
C	H	Q	Z	Y	W	H	N	H	Q
M	R	E	G	G	A	M	N	S	L
E	S	I	C	R	E	X	E	A	B
Y	A	P	U	K	W	P	H	W	D

Can you help sneezing Sally through the maze to find her box of tissues?

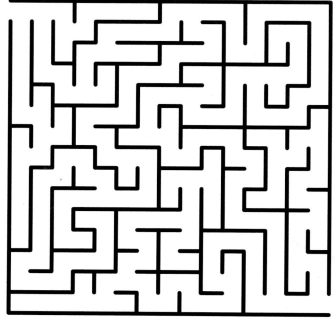

Turn to the next page to find the answers.

Answers

You should wash your hands...
✔ **A.** After going to the toilet

Germs can make you feel...
✔ **B.** Unwell

Which is the odd one out?
✔ **C.** Cheeseburger and chips

Vitamins are found naturally in...
✔ **A.** Fresh food

What would make you fitter?
✔ **B.** Playing chase with friends

Sleep helps you to...
✔ **A.** Refresh your body and mind

Y	S	H	Y	B	Y	D	R	D	F
R	H	N	T	L	H	A	B	I	T
H	S	T	I	A	T	O	C	H	U
Z	A	M	L	E	B	E	L	G	A
A	A	P	E	A	Q	M	E	N	I
F	O	T	P	V	E	O	A	I	I
C	H	Q	Z	Y	W	H	N	H	Q
M	R	E	G	G	A	M	N	S	L
E	S	I	C	R	E	X	E	A	B
Y	A	P	U	K	W	P	H	W	D

Well Done!
Now see how quickly you can fill your reward chart with stars by sticking to your healthy habits!